A souvenir guide

Glendurgan Garden
Cornwall

❊ National Trust

The Glory of Glendurgan

Glendurgan is a garden of dramatic contrasts with exotic plants set in deep Cornish valleys. Myriad greens from mosses, new foliage and grass banks contrast with a dazzling array of flowering plants. As you explore, glimpses within and beyond the garden are discovered.

Alfred Fox (1794–1874) came from a prosperous local family of ship agents, who benefited from the Packet Ship service that used Falmouth as a main port, handling mail from all over the world. In the 1820s Alfred became interested in acquiring property in this area. He laid out the main framework of the garden in the 1830s, developing it for the growing of fruit and vegetables as well as ornamental landscaping.

The garden was also intended as a space for his large family to enjoy. Its layout is highly individual and contains unique features such as the Maze and the Giant's Stride, adding real individuality as well as interest.

One of a kind

The ownership of Glendurgan by the Foxes for almost two centuries and the family's ongoing connection provide a remarkable continuity in the development of the garden. Successive generations of the family have contributed to creating this special garden. Today this gives us a garden full of character, in a magnificent setting.

Glendurgan is often compared to other gardens, however there can be few so connected to their origins. Comparisons are drawn because other gardens do a similar thing, not because Glendurgan attempts to copy any other valley garden in Cornwall.

This guidebook has been created to give a sense of both the development and key elements of the garden, and to share with you the best it has to offer throughout the seasons.

Left Forms of *Aquilegia vulgaris* have naturalised in the grassy meadows all around the garden

Right A spectacular autumn view

The Fox family

The Fox family was very influential in the area, living and working in Falmouth and the surrounding district. Alfred and his business partners had many links with the fishing villages along the coast of Cornwall, as fishing was one of their business interests.

Alfred's first investment in the area was the rental of fish cellars and several productive orchards behind the village of Durgan. As devout Quakers, the Foxes led lives that kept them in touch with the natural world and gardening for pleasure and sustenance was part of that. In 1826, with business booming and an expanding family, Alfred created a second home and built a thatched cottage at the top of the main valley above Durgan, establishing the beginnings of the garden we know today.

Room to grow

In 1837, Alfred was having lunch in Falmouth when news reached him that his cottage had burnt to the ground. According to Alfred's nephew Barclay (another keen gardener and fortunately for us also a diarist), Alfred burst out laughing, delighted that the apparent disaster had solved a problem he was in the midst of discussing – the accommodation of his ever-increasing family.

The new house was rebuilt on a larger scale, and was further extended by Alfred's son George (1845–1931) in 1891. In 1829, Alfred's wife Sarah (1804–90) started and ran the first school in Mawnan Smith parish. The school flourished until 1842 when it was closed. In 1876 a more permanent school was then built in Durgan (now a holiday cottage).

Above The original thatched cottage built in 1826

Opposite The house (not open to the public) that replaced the cottage at the head of the valley

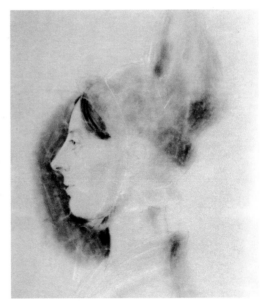

Foxes and the future

In December 1923 George Fox wrote that Glendurgan 'has been so enjoyed and loved by father and mother's descendants that it seems almost a family duty to carry on there as a family home if possible in the hope of future generations being privileged and able to do the same'.

It was perhaps for these reasons that his son and daughter-in-law, Cuthbert and Moyra Fox, and their son, Philip, decided to give the garden to the National Trust in 1962, the year of the bicentenary of the family firm, G. C. Fox & Co. Their foresight made it possible not only for Charles Fox and his family to continue the spirit of innovation and conservation begun by Alfred Fox, but also for generations of gardeners and visitors to enjoy the special character of this garden.

Top Alfred Fox

Above Sarah Fox, Alfred's wife

The origins of the garden

Little is known about the land before the arrival of the Foxes. On a map dated 1842 it is possible to identify the ancient field boundaries dotted around the garden, demonstrating a preference among the Foxes for keeping such characterful features. The next surviving map, dated 1880, shows extensive plantings of new trees and orchards.

Alfred and Sarah cleared the three valleys, which must have been overgrown and partly marshy farmland. In the 1830s they developed orchards and vegetable-growing areas to feed their expanding family (they went on to have 12 children). The main pond in the centre of the garden was dug and stocked with trout. At around the same time they started the development of the windbreaks that would both shelter the garden in later years and also create the view from the house. These trees included lime, beech, pine, oak, holm oak and a range of newly introduced North American conifers. Many of the large trees in the garden still originate from this era.

Growing and developing

By the time Alfred's son George took over Glendurgan in the 1890s, the framework of the garden was clearly established, and George was content to add ornamental trees and shrubs, as well as to carry on cultivating fruit trees. He was a keen botanist and naturalist, and grew hundreds of varieties of apples and pears as well as soft fruits, nectarines, peaches, figs, greengages and citrus fruits.

These fruit plantings are no longer present, however in recent years the garden team has carried out several plantings in the spirit of growing edible fruits. Firstly in the early 1990s the Olive Grove was established, and other interesting fruits have been added to that area including loquat, kiwi fruit and pecan nuts. In 2010 the plantation behind was cleared out and a range of Cornish apples planted. Additionally in the Cherry Orchard many new cherry trees have now been planted. Lastly the Glendurgan garden team also now has several good plantings of bananas.

Left View across the valley towards the now enormous Tulip Tree planted by Alfred Fox

Above A watercolour by Rachel Elizabeth Fox of a view of the Helford river from the house in the 1860s

Above right Flowering cherry tree in April

Sizeable fruit
The Fox family liked to record their success in growing fruit. In 1831 Alfred noted that he had 'gathered a gooseberry 4¼ inches [10.6 cm] in circumference'. In 1897 George wrote: 'Billy brought in citrus; one measured 1' 10" round the long way and 1' 9" the short way (the waist). It would just squeeze into my hat endways but would not go in the long way.'

A setting unlike any other

The garden is set on the Helford river and takes full advantage of the area's natural topography. The house (not open) is set at the head of the main valley, which descends steeply to the Helford below.

Either side of the main valley are paths that lead into two subsidiary valleys. To the north is the Cherry Orchard and then to the south is Birch's Orchard. Hidden below the tree line, giving an element of surprise as you explore the garden, lies the village of Durgan, a hamlet of 16 Cornish cottages with its own beach. Some of the cottages are owned by the National Trust, and several are available as holiday cottages.

In all weathers

The climate in comparison to other parts of the country is mild, wet and windy. Cornwall also benefits from the Gulf Stream. This and the prevailing southwesterly winds help to ensure that the worst of the Northern European winter weather does not reach Cornwall.

Generally the garden benefits from these conditions allowing us to grow an incredible range of plants. However those which prefer our conditions are usually from the wetter parts of Asia, rather than drier climates such as Mexico and South Africa.

Right An aerial view of Durgan village with the garden behind it

Far right Another watercolour by Rachel Elizabeth Fox from the 1860s showing the protective windbreak of trees

Planting and planning

Over many generations full advantage has been taken of the microclimates in the garden, allowing special plants seldom seen elsewhere to flourish here. There is also a range of habitats in the garden, from the dampest woodland glen to the driest Mediterranean bank. These again provide ideal conditions where more diverse plantings can be developed. The valley has never been drained and in many of the lower areas there are natural bogs, which allow for unusual plantings.

The natural profile of the valleys gives protection to the core of the garden. However it is the trees which have been successively planted around the boundaries which shelter the garden from the worst of the winds. The National Trust has substantially added to these to ensure that the garden is protected in future years, as many of the older trees are now reaching the end of their useful lives.

The view into the valley to the Helford river beyond

A garden of contrasts

The main aesthetic element to Glendurgan is contrast, the most fundamental of which being the natural Cornish setting, including the undulating wildflower banks, set against individual and quite often striking manmade features, such as the Maze.

The garden is shut in the winter, and the combination of the hard work of the garden team and gallons of rain and successions of winter storms ensures that come the spring everything is pristine and clean. The showiness of the camellias and magnolias then contrast with the understated beauty of the Cornish setting, as the mosses drip with water and the streams run fresh and clear.

Different textures

The wildflower banks are one of the key features of the garden. These areas provide contrast with the more exotic, introduced plants. Considerable time and thought are given to the spacing and placing of plants to ensure respect to each is given. The same open spaces also create some of the more arresting views in the garden.

The other key element to the wildflower areas is that they provide continuity for the eye, linking the different areas of the garden, their finer textures allowing the more dramatic foliage to express its full potential.

Worlds apart

The nature of the garden means that you become totally immersed in the deep valleys. This, combined with the different moods, means that the senses are constantly challenged. Cool shady areas contrast with open sunny spaces. The New Zealand area is shady and cool, so a range of plants which like these conditions has been used, including many large-leaved foliage plants which grow in antipodean forests. Contrasting with this, Bhutan is an open, sunny and warm area, and here we are cultivating conifers, rhododendrons and a range of other plants that enjoy such conditions.

Enjoyment and drama

Manmade features such as summerhouses and seats and swings add further interest, and remind the visitor that this was, and still is,

a family garden. The most notable feature at Glendurgan is of course the Maze (see over).

The introduction of large North American conifers such as the Western red cedar (*Thuja plicata*) has had a considerable impact on the garden. More recent plantings have seen introductions from the Edinburgh Conifer Conservation Programme. New conifers such as the Himalayan cypress (*Cupressus corneyana*) with its graceful blue foliage add much character to the plantings. An element that is very familiar in Glendurgan and other Fox gardens is the purple beech (*Fagus sylvatica purpurea*). These would have been extremely glamorous plants at the time they were introduced to the garden. In recent years many more introductions of exciting new plants have come into Cornish gardens, and they are being used wherever possible.

Left A view into valley of rhododendrons framed by the trunks of tree ferns (*Dicksonia antarctica*)

Above left Glendurgan is full of distinctive features that set it apart from other Cornish gardens

Above Yellow *Primula helodoxa* and rusty-leaved rodgersias

That amazing maze

This famous feature was created by Alfred Fox in 1833 to entertain family and friends. The design was taken from that of a maze at Sydney Gardens, Bath's oldest park.

The Sydney Gardens maze was laid out by the architect Harcourt Masters in 1795 and was on a flat site and much larger (covering 12 acres [4.9 hectares]). At that time it was thought to be the oldest complete informal hedge maze in the country. It became very popular towards the end of the 18th century and was frequently visited by members of the royal family and the author Jane Austen, who lived at No. 4 Sydney Place.

So many aspects

Alfred cleverly used the east-facing slope to position his maze. This means that there are exceptional views from various lookouts facing west from Manderson's Hill. The Maze is certainly a sight to behold: from a distance it looks like a tea plantation in Assam; studied in detail the intriguing shapes create patterns like fingerprints. However it was designed not only to be wondered at but also to be wandered in, so take the opportunity to do both.

The design of the Glendurgan maze varies slightly from the original: at the centre of each quarter of the original maze was a summerhouse; in today's maze there is a C-shaped hedge with a Chusan palm (*Trachycarpus fortunei*) at its centre. Instead

A few facts and figures
Total length of paths including
all dead ends – 706 metres.
Total distance to the centre
of the Maze – 374.5 metres.
Total number of strides to the
centre of the Maze – 749 metres.

of the grotto in the original design, there is
a timber-framed thatched summerhouse.

Planting and puzzling

In 1833 the Maze was intended to be fun for
family and friends; no thought would have
been given to the very different way it is used
today. The hedges are common laurel and
thought to be the same as those used for the
maze at Sydney Gardens. The biggest
challenge at Glendurgan is the fact that the
lower section is planted on a bog. Although
there are drawbacks to using laurel for hedges,
in these boggy conditions nothing else would
survive. In unusually cool and wet years the
Maze can struggle and turn yellow in places.
Extensive work has been done to drain these
sections but it is an ongoing challenge.

Left An aerial view
of the maze

Above left An old guide
to the maze in Sydney
Gardens, Bath, which
provided the model for
the Glendurgan maze

Top The Maze takes four
people three days to cut
and is cut twice a year

Above The Maze during
restoration in 1991

A high-maintenance hedge

Another challenging aspect of the Maze is
the surface area that is created by all the
hedges. This makes the Maze an incredibly
labour-intensive feature to look after. Each year
we strive to prune sections of the hedges to
keep them vigorous and stop them becoming
woody. Additionally we have had to hand
weed to keep the base of the hedges clean.

In 1991 the Maze was in a really poor
condition and a decision was taken to restore it.
The hedges were cut to ground level, the path
surfaces were reinstated and the summerhouse
added. Although a difficult decision at the time,
it has resulted in a maze in very good health.

Magnificent magnolias

Magnolias are without doubt the most majestic of all flowering temperate trees and shrubs. Amongst this large group of plants the large-flowered Asiatics stand out as the showiest of all.

The garden is well suited to these for many reasons. Firstly, frost not only damages flowers but also kills young trees as they come into growth. However in the garden's mild conditions, most years this is avoided. Secondly, they love a deep, moist root run and again the conditions in the valley are perfect

for them. Most importantly, to the visitor at least, is the opportunity to display them to their best advantage: the steep paths and views along and across the valleys allow these spectacular flowers to be viewed and admired in a variety of ways.

Fabulous flowers

The Asiatic species – including *M. campbellii*, *M. sprengeri* and *M. sargentiana robusta* – are often the first to flower and the ones with the largest flowers. The large pink, mauve or white tepals (see box) produce flowers of

Magnolia anatomy

A tepal is a part of the outer part of a flower in which the petals and sepals are of similar shape and colour, or undifferentiated, and therefore cannot be easily distinguished from one another. Petals are modified leaves that surround the reproductive parts of flowers. They are often brightly coloured or unusually shaped to attract pollinators. Usually green, sepals form the outermost whorl of, and function as protection for, the flower in bud, often providing support for the petals when in bloom.

M. campbellii var. *mollicomata*. This plant comes from Yunnan, a mountainous province in southern China, making it a hardier form than others

dinner-plate proportions, usually starting in February at Glendurgan.

The flower buds are fascinating too, wrapped up in their hairy coats. These buds patiently sit, waiting for the temperature to rise and the day length to increase. Then suddenly the first flower comes out and gradually, one by one, each tree will be covered in these incredible flowers, balanced like blousy ballerinas on bare branches. Many are quite rare in the wild now, as the trees are often harvested and the buds used for medicinal purposes.

So very varied

Next to mention are the pure whites of *M. kobus*, *M. stellata* and *M. denudata*. These are the less showy varieties but so reliable that they flower well most years. *M. stellata* is a treasure with its many tepals, often on small trees. *Denudata* with its goblet-shaped ivory-white flowers is one of the very best magnolias to see each spring, set at the head of Cherry Orchard.

The later plants with pink and purple flowers are *M.* x *soulangeana* types. Originally a French hybrid, these are good, reliable garden plants which flower for a very long period and can repeat flower in mid-summer.

Lastly, the garden has a set of evergreen species, the best of which is the magnificent *M. doltsopa* with large, creamy and strongly scented flowers. The collection also includes the relatively newly introduced *M. laevifolia*. This species with neat, cream, small flowers originates from China and prefers to grow in open sunny places.

Far left A view of a magnolia tree in bud in early spring

Below left *M. campbellii* var. *alba*. In the wild the most common form is white, however most in cultivation are pink

Above left *M. sargentiana robusta alba*. With dramatic, large flowers, this plant is very rare in cultivation

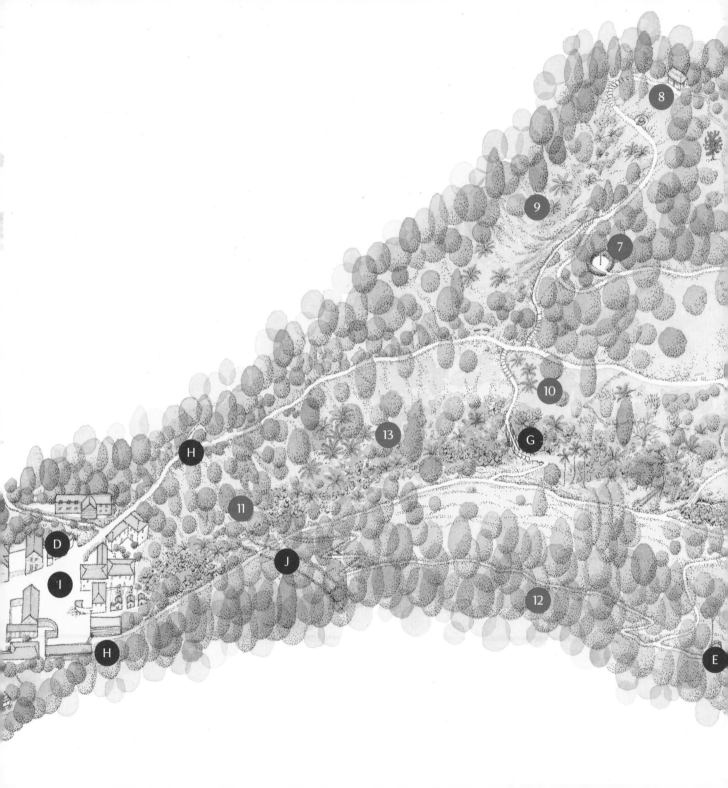

Tour of the Garden

We very much hope you will enjoy your visit. There are so many things to see, in your own time and at your own pace. There's no order that's best but, for the first-time visitor, we recommend following the numbered route. At Manderson's Hill (number 12) you can choose whether to take a longer walk along the higher path, or follow the main route past the Jungle (number 13).

Giant's Stride

The Fish Pond

The beach at Durgan

The view from Manderson's Hill

Highlights of Glendurgan

There are fine specimens all over, collected from all corners of the globe. It would be impossible to list all the spectacular species this garden is proud to cultivate, so here are just a few of our finest. We've numbered the highlights to show you in which area you can find them on the map (open to see).

Stan Shebs

Saxifraga stolonifera

National Trust/Carole Drake

Grevillea barklyana

Moraea huttonii

National Trust/Carole Drake

GAP Photos Ltd/S&O

Watsonia 'Stanford Scarlet'

Tasmanian flax-lily (*Dianella tasmanica*)

GAP Photos Ltd/Jenny Lilly

National Trust/Carole Drake

Rhaphiolepis umbellata

GAP Photos Ltd/Geoff Kidd

Camellia 'Cornish Snow'

Agave americana

National Trust

National Trust/Carole Drake

Puya chilensis

4 Banana plants (*Musa basjoo*) and Arum lilies

National Trust/Hannah Atkinson

4 Rice-paper plant (*Tetrapanax papyrifera*)

National Trust/Carole Drake

9 *Hypericum* 'Rowallene'

GAP Photos Ltd/Dave Bevan

13 Ginger lily (*Hedychium* x *raffillii*)

GAP Photos Ltd/Dave Bevan

10 Silver tree fern (*Cyathea dealbata*)

GAP Photos Ltd/S&O

13 Chilean fire tree (*Embothrium coccineum*)

National Trust Images/Paul Mogford

13 Red root (*Wachendorfia thyrsiflora*)

GAP Photos Ltd/Visions

14 Jelly palm (*Butia capitata*)

National Trust/Tamsin Hennah

14 Chusan palm (*Trachycarpus fortunei*)

National Trust Images/Andrew Lawson

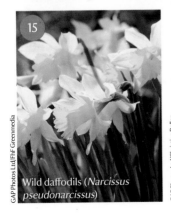

15 Wild daffodils (*Narcissus pseudonarcissus*)

GAP Photos Ltd/FhF Greenmedia

15 *Rhododendron* x *loderi*

GAP Photos Ltd/Christina Bollen

15 Tulip tree (*Liriodendron tulipifera*)

National Trust Images/David Sellman

Key

A   Main entrance

B   Car park

C   Garden entrance building and shop

D   Toilets/Durgan WC

E   Viewing platform

F   Boat Seat

G   Bamboo Bridge

H   Access to Durgan

I   Durgan Village

J   Old cattle rush

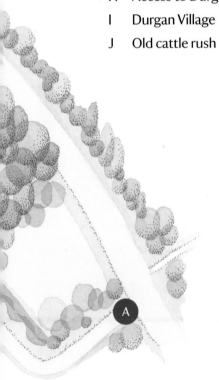

The Garden Entrance and the Camellia Walk

The first section of the garden is relatively new, planted on either side with a range of sun-loving plants. One of the great feature plants of Glendurgan for many years has been the *Agave americana*, also known as the century plant (see centre spread). These huge plants take many years to flower, although not as long as their common name would suggest. These are surrounded by carpets of low, spreading plants such as thrift and *Geranium* 'Tanya Rendall'.

Other plants include grevilleas, which have flowers like coiled-up springs. The smallest is the flat, red-flowered *Grevillea lanigera* and the most flamboyant is *G. barklyana*, or the toothbrush grevillea, with purple-red spikes (see centre spread). Amongst these are two South African restios, *Elegia capensis* and *Cannomois virgata*, which grows three to four metres tall. In the summer a range of South African bulbous plants add colour, including *Watsonia* 'Stanford Scarlet' (see centre spread),

Tritonia rosea, the pineapple flower spikes of eucomis and dierama (Angel's fishing rod).

As the entrance path merges into the 19th-century Camellia Walk, the plantings change to a woodland type. Amongst the array of camellias are tender varieties, including the rich waxy flowers in April of reticulatas 'Purple Gown' and 'Captain Rawes'. The earliest to flower each year is *Camellia* 'Cornish Snow', a simple white (see centre spread). 'Winton' and 'Cornish Spring'

are similar. In recent years more unusual hybrids and species have been introduced to diversify the plantings, including a few of the winter-flowering *Camellia sasanqua*. Camellias clearly dominate here but there are others that vie for attention. Rhododendrons include the scented white 'Lady Alice Fitzwilliam', 'Fragrantissima', the magenta 'Cornish Red' and 'Cynthia'. In mid-summer two eucryphia flower, *Eucryphia lucida* 'Pink Cloud' and *E. moorei*.

Above **The Camellia Walk**

Above left *Camellia* 'Inspiration' on the Camellia Walk in April

Below left **The foxes at the visitor entrance are a re-creation of the originals, which came from the Foxes' Falmouth townhouse**

Right **Angel's fishing rod, or dierama**

The Valley Head Path and the Fish Pond

For the best route go straight on at the junction and follow the Valley Head Path, which links the two sides of the main valley and offers one of the best sites for Mediterranean planting.

In 2012 Ned Lomax from the garden team went to South Africa and the Drakensberg Mountains, where the climate is similar to Cornwall – cool and wet. The heathers from this region have much more exotic flowers than the diminutive European species, and from this expedition Ned brought back *Erica discolor* and *E. verticillata*.

Further along, the true nature of the garden reveals itself, as the grass banks fall away and the valley opens out, revealing the view down to the Helford river.

On the far side of this valley is a collection of local rhododendron hybrids, many from the Foxes' other gardens. These were bred from the plants brought back on J. D. Hooker's famous expedition to Sikkim in 1849. They include the much-admired 'Barclayi' and 'Penjerrick'.

On the higher side of the path are puyas, dramatic, spiky plants which originate from Chile and are related to the pineapple (see *Puya chilensis*, centre spread). The crowns of strap-shaped leaves are quite brutal-looking, with inward- and outward-facing hooks. The

flower spikes erupt out of the crowns in May and can grow up to three metres in height. These subdivide horizontally into perches, so birds can sit and feed on the nectar and in turn pollinate the flowers.

This path culminates with the Fish Pond. The conditions here allow for the best growing conditions in the garden, and the bananas flower most years. Three different tree ferns grow here, including on the left (or south) side a New Zealand species, *Dicksonia squarrosa*. Orchids and other epiphytes are being grown on the tree fern trunks. A great semi-shade-loving ground cover plant found here is *Saxifraga stolonifera* (see centre spread), which has white flowers in early June.

On leaving this area via the steps, turn right. The plants on either side of this path are dominated by a collection of rhododendrons, including *Rhododendron* x *loderi* (see centre spread) and the tender *Rhododendron dalhousiae* (May) with large lily-like flowers.

Left top *Erica discolor*

Left below *Erica verticillata*

Right The trunk of Prickly Moses (*Acacia verticillata*) surrounded by bluebells and wild garlic (*Allium ursinum*)

Far right *Rhododendron dalhousiae*

The Holy Bank

Mounds of flowering rhododendrons frame the view down the Valley Head Path towards the Helford river

This is a Victorian feature, particularly appropriate in the garden of a Quaker family. Plants include the Tree of Heaven (*Ailanthus altissima*), Judas tree (*Cercis siliquastrum*), Crown of Thorns (*Colletia cruciata*), Prickly Moses (*Acacia verticillata*) and the Glastonbury thorn (*Crataegus monogyna* 'Biflora').

Walking on, a framed glimpse through the dark green Irish yews shows off the luxuriant Canary Island palms (*Phoenix canariensis*). The banks looking down over the Maze give a sense of the dramatic topography of the garden. In spring they are covered in wildflowers, including primroses, violets, orchids, bluebells and columbines. This supports a rich insect population, including oil beetles and butterflies.

Continue along the path until it turns to the left. Turn right here and take the path through the Olive Grove, and other recently planted curiosities, such as loquats, Asian pears and kiwi fruits. These form a link between the garden's fruit-growing origins and a new apple orchard to the west. Underneath the huge Monterey pine, *Cyclamen coum* and *Iris reticulata* flower in the spring.

The alternative route is to head straight to the Giant's Stride. On your left is perhaps the best internal view, looking north-east across to the far side of the valley, the multitude of trees contrasting with each other and changing through the seasons.

On the side of the path in the spring is the Widow iris (*Hermodactylus tuberosa*) with its black flowers. Both paths, either through the Olive Grove or past the Giant's Stride, will take you to the School Room.

The Giant's Stride, more commonly known as a maypole, is another unusual feature. It was installed in 1913 on a plot of land which had previously been a croquet ground.

The School Room sits at the head of the valley. The original building was constructed by the family in 1829, and was used by Sarah Fox until 1842. When the School Room was re-created in 2001 Charles and Caroline Fox were involved in its design. Today it links with the past, but also provides an interesting feature in the garden as well as shelter from any downpours – not uncommon Cornish occurrences.

Birch's Orchard

This western valley is smaller and more intimate than the other valleys as it opens out from below. The mature trees with underplanted laurel are critical as shelter to the garden. In the early days of the garden this was an orchard and is named after a former tenant, Mr Birch.

Yellow Skunk cabbage is the first to flower and thrives in the damp conditions beside the stream. Hypericums have been used throughout the valley, including 'Hidcote' and the taller 'Rowallene' (see centre spread). The dainty *Hypericum uralum* is a hardy Chinese species and is planted in several places. These are often contrasted with hydrangeas, particularly the small, intensely blue *Hydrangea serrata* 'Blue Tit'.

Two conifers have been planted: the pendulous *Cupressus corneyana*, or walking-stick tree, comes from Bhutan where, according to legend, it sprouted from the walking stick planted by Guru Rinpoche, who introduced Buddhism to Bhutan; the other on the far bank is *Taiwania cryptomerioides*, a slow-growing tree whose timber is used for temples and coffins. Both are very elegant, weeping conifers with blue foliage. Other plants include a range of rhododendrons with yellow flowers, from the small early *Rhododendron lutescens* to the large-flowered *Rhododendron macabeanum* from India.

Turn right to walk down the steps through Birch's Orchard and this will lead you to the area known as New Zealand.

Above The School Room at the head of Birch's Orchard

Above far left *Cyclamen coum* in the Olive Grove in February

Above left The black-edged flowers of the Widow iris make an early appearance in spring

Left Also early-flowering, *Iris reticulata* has deep velvety-blue flowers with a darker shade on the lower petals

New Zealand and Bhutan

Top *Rhododendron kesangiae*

Above The toothed lancewood is native to New Zealand

The idea of planting areas with a geographical theme was first developed in the mid-1990s. The inspiration for Bhutan came from a trip made at that time by John Sales, the National Trust's then Chief Gardens Adviser, and also a visit which Charles Fox made to the Himalayas in the early 1980s. They could sense that with careful thought, plantings could be developed to capture the character of that dramatic region. Material was amassed including the large-leaved, ivory flowered *Rhododendron grande*, the early scarlet-flowered *R. barbatum* and the later *R. thomsonii*, plus a new species, *R. kesangiae*, which was named after Kesang, Queen of Bhutan from 1952 to 1972. In 2012 further thinning and plantings were made, including the remarkable *R. lindleyi* with scented white flowers balancing on the ends of the twigs.

The New Zealand area was developed to capture the spirit of this country's unique flora, dominated by massive conifers, the most impressive being the kauris (*Agathis australis*). These, as well as many of the other trees and shrubs, have curious brown, dead-looking leaves, especially *Pseudopanax ferox*. Ferns are a significant part of the flora of New Zealand: the iconic *Cyathea dealbata* (the silver tree fern, see centre spread) has become an international emblem of New Zealand, especially in the sporting world.

The Lower Valley, The Jungle

Quercus rubra

Hydrangea aspera

The Bamboo Bridge links New Zealand and Bhutan with the Jungle

From here go down the main path, following the ancient boundary wall. Glimpses open out between the trees to the sunnier side of the valley. Plants of note include the cream-flowered evergreen *Magnolia doltsopa* in late March, *Quercus rubra*, one of the American red oaks and the soft pastel-pink lace-caps of *Hydrangea aspera* in August. After a huge windbreak of Portuguese laurel (*Prunus lusitanica*), the last section of the garden is kept simply to blue hydrangeas and white rhododendrons, 'Polar Bear' and *auriculatum*.

Go through the gate and enjoy the village of Durgan, before returning via the gate on the east side. Here the woodland setting is interspersed with very tall *Abies alba*, the European silver fir, which thrives in the mild climate. Under these are two parallel walls, an ancient cattle rush, where the cows would have been allowed to come down to drink water from the stream.

At this point it is possible to go up the steps to your right through the wooded areas to the top of Manderson's Hill for a view down into the garden. This is worthwhile in the late spring when the bluebells are in flower. The maze-viewing platform is found further along this path (point E on the map in the centrefold).

The Jungle

If not taking the woodland path, follow the main path into the Jungle. Here the feeling of the tropics comes from the bold foliage of bananas, giant rhubarb and other exotic flowering plants. *Wachendorfia thyrsiflora* (see centre spread) from South Africa has leaves that look as if they have been concertinaed and a spike of yellow flowers in April. These are followed by ginger lilies, including *Hedychium* x *raffillii* (see centre spread) with blue-green leaves.

On the higher side of the bank a few feature plants have been placed, including the graceful and tender *Juania australis* (Chonta palm), which originates from the Pacific Ocean. A little further on, a path leads back to the Bamboo Bridge (point G on the centrefold map) and New Zealand and Bhutan. On the bank adjacent to this path is the Chilean fire tree, or *Embothrium coccineum* (see centre spread), which has bright red flowers in late spring.

The Maze and the Pond

You will soon reach the centre of the garden, where you will see the Maze and Pond. Note the conifers that are used extensively in the garden to create structure. In recent years many have come from Edinburgh Botanic Garden, where they are carefully conserved by scientists.

On the lower side of the path are the remains of a giant Western red cedar (*Thuja plicata*). The root plate of this tree started to loosen, so it was winched out in 2012. The remaining sections are layers from this tree, where the tips of the branches have rooted and grown into new trees.

Next the path splits, either down to the Maze and Pond, or carrying on up the hill to another viewing point.

The Pond was originally stocked with trout. Today it is an important central feature, and the planting is designed to give an ornamental feel. In the surrounding area notable trees include three cunninghamias – a conifer that likes a moist atmosphere – and a large deciduous conifer, *Taxodium distichum* from North America. The magnolia next to the Pond is *M. sargentiana robusta alba*.

Continue along the path with the Maze and Pond to your left to reach the Cherry Orchard.

Above **The Maze seen from across the Pond**

The Cherry Orchard

This is the last main section of the garden. Here many of the plants have white flowers. This colour theme originates from the cherry trees planted by Alfred Fox when it was a productive garden. Where he planted edible cherries, today there are ornamental ones, which look their best in April. Here in the damp deep soils magnolias thrive, and herbaceous plants in the boggy sections include Rodgersia, the Japanese flag (*Iris ensata*) and early in the year snowdrops and snowflakes (*Leucojum vernum*), a native bulb.

At the head of this valley is the Boat Seat. This was inspired by the story that Alfred Fox kept his gardening tools under a boat. When this was first developed as a feature, the bow of a rowing boat was used. However, when that began to succumb to the damp climate, a local craftsman, David Hart, was commissioned to make a seat in the style of a boat in materials less susceptible to rot.

Continue along the path up the hill and you come to a fork in the path. The left-hand path will take you back down to the Maze, passing the huge tulip tree, thought to have been planted in the 1830s. Apart from flowering well each year in July, these trees also put on a remarkable display of autumnal colour.

Taking the right-hand path at the fork will lead you back to the Camellia Walk and exit.

Below Magnolias in April framing the upturned boat seat in the Cherry Orchard

Glendurgan Today

The way the wildflower banks change sums up how the garden and the seasons change at Glendurgan. In early spring they are like tidy blankets of velvet. As the wildflowers grow, the textures and colours stir into life with bright flowers appearing everywhere. Summer sees the grass cut and the bold tropical foliage plants taking centre stage. By October the green has returned, covered by the colours of falling autumn leaves.

Spring
Sights and smells

Spring comes early to Glendurgan with light and long days, a frost-free climate and a sheltered valley where cold air drains out to the sea. In the early spring, violets and primroses can be found in the hedges alongside abundant rhododendrons and camellias in bloom. Many magnificent magnolias are in flower. Later, wild garlic and beautiful bluebells scent the air, and aquilegias and native orchids fill the valley banks.

Summer
Shapes and sounds

Although summer is not the main season at Glendurgan, there is still a range of garden gems from tiny seeds to giant trees. Summer breaks in a wave of whiteness with the eucryphia in flower. Mighty giants make interesting shapes, like the tulip trees in flower, the delicate leaves of the handkerchief tree and the umbrella canopy of the gunnera.

At the same time the wildlife comes alive, with dragonflies and damselflies beating their wings by the pond and birds and bees humming above the valley banks. The exotic bamboos, banana plants, ferns and palms also present textures and shapes of interest.

Autumn
A feast of colour

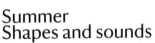

Trees, old and familiar, great and majestic, native and exotic, dominate the autumn landscape. The feast of colour is provided by copper beech, weeping swamp cypress, dawn redwood and a range of evergreens. Drama is provided by the changing colours and contrasting shades of their foliage against the valley backdrop. The tulip trees in particular look stunning and the unusual Katsura tree also provides striking colour with a sweet candyfloss scent in the autumn months.

Above left The magnolias offer a spectacular show after the long winter months

Above right By early summer, the rhododendron petals are falling but the gunnera is surging upwards

The tulip tree aflame with autumn colour

From the gardening team

'The terrain and the style of the garden have a profound effect on both the equipment we use and the type of gardening we do. It is not a garden for the light-hearted. I often say it is "off-road gardening" because of the terrain and how physically demanding it is.' Here, according to Garden Manager John Lanyon, are some of the challenges and rewards of gardening at Glendurgan.

'There are no flower borders here as in most gardens but acres of natural meadow. These need strimming and raking off and all the grass removed twice a year. As with all passionate gardening teams, ours strives to show the garden at its best every day. Ben Tufnell has

worked in the garden for many years, and every day he sets up a new work programme to accomplish what is best for the garden.

'The garden has been hugely invested into since the storm of 1990. Head Gardener Rob James built a partnership with John Sales and Peter Mansfield, and between them the garden was seriously upgraded and this work still carries on today. Both the plantings and the garden features are in a very good condition and this is down to the passion of everyone involved with the property, all carried out in a very professional and warm-hearted spirit.

'Challenges with pests and diseases mean the garden and plantings have to change, but we are trying to manage and understand them. The better we garden, the better plant health we have and often this means we will be successful. We are recording and propagating our old plants, but we are also introducing and experimenting with new ones. There is no better example of this than our experiments with epiphytes – plants that grow on other plants. Our damp and humid climate means that it is worth us trying to do this. If you look around you will see ferns, orchids,

Above left Crocosmia may look attractive but it is the bane of the gardeners' lives

Left Epiphytes grow on other plants in the wild without doing them any harm

rhododendrons and other plants growing on trees. They do not hurt the trees in any way, and this is in fact what happens in the wild.

'The meadows of wildflowers are the garden's main feature, so we try really hard to care for them. To make our life easier and improve the effect of the meadows, we are using semi-parasitic plants such as lousewort and yellow rattle. These cleverly live on the roots of the grasses reducing their vigour, leaving us with less to cut and pick up. Our

worst enemy is montbretia, or crocosmia. This was planted in the past but today has become an almost indestructible weed. We have to cut the banks earlier than we would like in order to prevent this plant spreading further.

'The garden has a strong spirit and it is wonderful to see the different elements contrast and complement one another. Each year when the velvet carpets of bluebells flower, it makes us very proud of all we have achieved.'

Above Gardening with the terrain for the most naturalistic feel

Durgan and North Helford

Durgan is an entry point to the Helford river – a beautiful area with peaceful, wooded creeks in the upper reaches and lovely coves and beaches nearer the mouth.

There are many walks with good links to the coast path, making it easy to create varied circular walks. Take in the dramatic scenery around Rosemullion Head and Toll Point, then drop down to the more sheltered shore and crystal-clear water of the river. Return through the dappled shade of woodland valleys at Carwinion and Nansidwell, or back across Bosloe hay meadows, rich in wildflowers and insects.

Much of the National Trust's land around the Helford was acquired during the 1930s when it was recognised that there was a threat to this landscape from expanding building developments. The National Trust continues to manage the area to maximize conservation benefit and protect rare species and habitats. For example, the land at Rosemullion Head is sensitively managed by the ranger team and tenant farmer to retain the herb-rich grassland, which makes it a botanically important site with a mix of coastal wildflowers including rare orchids.

Durgan is a quiet hamlet at the base of Glendurgan Garden, formerly a fishing village. Fish, and particularly shellfish, are still important industries of the river. In the village and along the Helford there are many picturesque holiday cottages and it is easy to spend a week's holiday here without using the car.

A view west up the Helford river